ANGELA'S KITCHEN
[IL-KĊINA TA' ANGELA]

PAUL CAPSIS, JULIAN MEYRICK AND HILARY BELL

CURRENCY PRESS
SYDNEY

GRIFFIN
THEATRE
COMPANY

CURRENT THEATRE SERIES

First published in 2012
by Currency Press Pty Ltd,
PO Box 2287, Strawberry Hills, NSW, 2012, Australia
enquiries@currency.com.au
www.currency.com.au

in association with Griffin Theatre Company, Sydney

Reprinted 2015, 2018

NATIONAL LIBRARY OF AUSTRALIA CIP DATA

Author:	Capsis, Paul.
Title:	Angela's kitchen / Paul Capsis, Julian Meyrick and Hilary Bell.
ISBN:	9780868199467 (pbk.)
Series:	Current theatre series.
Subjects:	Capsis, Paul.
	Immigrants—New South Wales—Sydney—Drama.
	Immigrants—New South Wales—Sydney—Biography.
	Maltese—Australia—Drama.
	Maltese—Australia—Biography.
Other Authors/Contributors:	
	Meyrick, Julian.
	Bell, Hilary.
Dewey Number:	A822.4

Contents

Typeset by Dean Nottle for Currency Press.
Cover photograph by Katie Kaars. Cover design by Interbrand.
Front cover shows Paul Capsis.

Currency Press acknowledges the Traditional Owners of the Country on
which we live and work. We pay our respects to all Aboriginal and Torres
Strait Islander Elders, past and present.

Angela's Kitchen was first produced by the Griffin Theatre Company at SBW Stables Theatre, Sydney, on 5 November 2010, with the following participants:

Performer, Paul Capsis

Director, Julian Meyrick
Associate Writer, Hilary Bell
Designer, Louise McCarthy
Lighting Designer, Verity Hampson
Music, Sound and AV Designer, Steve Toulmin

CHARACTERS

ANGELA and all other characters are played by the one performer.

SETTING

A cupboard, a table and two chairs. Some tins and kitchen items line the top of the cupboard.

NOTE ON TEXT

Double inverted commas indicate an internal thought, e.g., "Wow, that's so full-on Maltese".

Single inverted commas indicate reported dialogue, e.g.,'Look at her! Look what's she's doing! She crazy?'

Maltese language phrases are followed by the English translation in brackets if they appear without such translation in the spoken text, e.g., *'M'ghandekx issawwat it-tfal, m'ghandekx issawwat it-tfal tieghek'.* ['Mustn't hit kids, mustn't hit your children'.].

Translations in brackets are not intended to be spoken aloud.

All stage directions are drawn from the original Griffin production and are not intended to be binding.

A song plays: a Maltese lullaby.
Paul sings along with it.

Nan, Nan,
Orqod, orqod ibni orqod
Għandi ward u ġiżimin
Għandek ommok il-Madonna
U l-missierek il-Bambin

Nan, Nan,
Orqod, orqod ibni orqod
Biex ngħattik fix-xuguman
Mentri ma nistax norqod
Għax niftakar fil-musmar

Nan.

POSTCARD FROM MALTA I

Paul looks at the cupboard onstage.

I'm looking into the sky, the beautiful, immense, endless, endless blue Maltese sky. There is St Julian's Bay out over the water and I can see houses and boats. It is very hot today. The water is glistening and I look at the beautiful, old, waterfront dwellings, their sandstone practically white. It is siesta and very quiet. I can feel a breeze. I walk up the hill and at the top I see a big church, Kalkara, at the bottom Balluta Bay. There are hundreds of steps running around the edges of the coast road that disappear out of sight. On my left there is a beach with shops and alleyways around it. But I keep on the road. Ahead of me is a tall watchtower, distant and dark.

The road bends and twists. I can see a group of boys playing in the sand, shouting and laughing and swearing in Maltese. I can clearly see the watchtower now. There's a hotel. A big, modern one. A group of tourists come out, with bags. I wonder where all the little alleyways lead, where they go. I can see the tops of churches in the distance.

Now the road is open on my left and I can see the ocean. I'm nearly out of St Julian's and heading towards Sliema. *Karozzin* go past, taking sightseers around the city. When she was a girl, my grandmother used to jump on them and get rides, hanging on the back. It's so hot. I can hear the faint sound of bells. And I can see, down near the rocks, wooden pylons sticking out of the water. I remember my grandmother saying that in this part of Sliema, called Għar id-Dud, there was a nightclub wrecked by a wild storm, completely destroyed, and never repaired. I turn right, and take a road that, I'm pretty sure, will take me to Gżira where my grandmother lived. There are a lot more people—and noise. Suddenly, there's screaming. A guy gets out of his car and shouts in Maltese, *'Ħares lejha! Ħares lejn dak li qed tagħmel! Hija miġnuna?'* ['Look at her! Look what's she's doing! She crazy?'] A woman with blonde hair has driven up on the footpath and people are flying out of the way. *'Madonna! X'qed tagħmel? Hija miġnuna! Hija għaddejja biex toqtol xi ħadd! Oqgħod attenta, slut li int.'* ['Madonna! What is she doing? She's crazy! She's going to kill someone! Look out, slut that you are.'] Everyone is shouting, there are people coming out of shops, shouting. The woman takes off. And I'm, like, "Wow, that's so full-on Maltese".

I arrive on Cameron Street. The house was either number 86 or 68. It's a long street and stretches out ahead of me. If I look to the left I can see, way down, the Orpheum, the cinema my grandmother used to go to. It's still there. I look at the numbers on the houses, and I walk three blocks and I think I'm in front of my grandmother's house. I think it's number 86. I'm pretty sure it's number 86. *That's the house.* [*Photograph is shown.*] On the ground floor there are two sets of doors and between them an *anteporta*. One set is open and I can see there is a window with lace curtains. I want to go and look in, but I don't, in case someone's there. So I just look. For ages and ages and ages and ages and ages. And I think about my grandmother and my mother, born in that house, and the air raids. And I take lots of photographs of the house, opposite the house and next door to the house, alongside the house, along the street.

I walk away towards the Orpheum, and I think about my grandmother, and how many times she walked up and down this street with her children. Now I'm in front of the Orpheum and it's a *huge* building, art deco. It could be in 1941 because absolutely everything is preserved in time. I walk round the side and notice there's a door open and noise is coming from inside. I think, "What's going on, is there a movie playing?" I look in and it's *packed with women playing Bingo.* And they *all* look up and stare at me. And I think, "Oh my God, I'm actually standing in the cinema my grandmother has told me so much about".

THE HAIR STORY

St Peter's Parish Church is just around the corner from my grandmother's home, in Devonshire Street, Surry Hills. My brother and I walked there every Sunday. There are a lot of memories for me there. My grandfather's funeral was in that church, I was christened there, and my mother was attacked by my aunty in that church when I was five. I don't know why. My mother was with a girlfriend and they were giggling as we walked in. My aunt was walking behind us and I was mouthing off and saying silly things. Next thing, my aunty grabs my mother by the hair and starts pulling her through the church, swearing. I will never forget it. Mum was on the floor going, 'Let go, you fucking bitch'. I was hysterical. I screamed [*a scream*] and the priest said, 'Get that boy out of here, get that crying child out of here'.

EATING STONE

For my grandmother there were three big things: poverty, the War and coming to Australia. The Maltese village where she grew up was isolated, and they were really poor. When her mother died she was sent to live with a cousin in Gżira.

She was not allowed to go to school. She had to work. She never learnt to read and write. She would sit outside the school and watch the kids inside. She talked about the poverty. One of her sisters was so hungry, she would go behind the church and scrape off the limestone and eat it. By the time they realised what was happening she was gone.

She had lots of brothers and sisters, but only three survived. Her mother died at 38, in childbirth. Angela was eight. She and her older brother Tony walked all the way from their village to see her, laid out on the hospital table, the dead baby beside her. Her brother told her, *'Int ma għandekx permess tibki'*. 'You are not allowed to cry'. *'Int ma għandekx permess tibki.'*

Then Angela's father went to live with her maternal aunt. They stayed in the village and he worked. He never gave Angela any money. She would say to me, *'F'din il-ħajja ħadd ma jagħti xejn, lanqas missierek'*. 'In this life no-one will ever give anything, not even your own father'. He died the year before she came to Australia.

RETURN TO MALTA

When I was flying in from London I saw the entire island. "I know Malta is small but it is not possible to see the whole island from a plane." I thought, "That can't be it, that's not Malta, that might be a bit of Malta". But it was all of it. The next thing we landed at St Lucca and came through Customs and there was a man the spitting image of Lonz. The hat, the face, the clothes. "Oh my God, it's my grandfather." A younger version, there at the airport. I rang my grandmother to say I had arrived in Malta. She had forgotten to tell me about her cousin she lived with when she was eight. I said, 'But, Nan, she lives just around the corner'. And it was extraordinary. I knocked on the door and said, 'Hi, I am Paul from Australia… I am related to…' *'Idħol!* Come in!', and she was crying and, 'You're just like a son to me. Come and visit us every time you are in Malta.'

THE BOMBINGS

During World War Two Malta was the most bombed place on earth. Over two years, there were 3,000 air raids. In one six-month period, there was only one day without an air raid. Bombs destroyed 35,000 buildings. Thousands were killed, wounded, left homeless.

The first time I went to Malta, I went to the suburb Angela lived in during the War. The first air raid in Malta was in that street. A little boy was killed. Angela said they always knew whether it was the Germans bombing or the Italians. The bombing was heavy in the German raids but with the Italians... very soft. You'd hear the air raid siren and run to the shelter and would hardly hear a thing. The Italians dropped their bombs in the water. They wouldn't drop them on a Catholic country.

Pause.

Angela told me that because my grandfather was a carpenter he made shelves for everybody in the shelter. Everyone had their corners and he built little beds off the ground. But he never would stay in the shelter, my grandfather. The men never stayed in the shelter. They'd watch the bombing from their *bait*. In Malta the roofs are flat and they would watch from their *bait*.

THE KITCHEN EXPLAINED

Angela never sat down at the table when we ate. It was always my brother, me and my grandfather. I'll describe the table. For my grandfather, we didn't exist unless we made noise and then it would be, 'Hey, be quiet!' It was rare for my mother to join us but when she did she would be here. 'Don't make a mess. Manuel, eat it, you are too skinny, eat it. I'm going out with Lizzie tonight so youse two better not misbehave, I don't want to hear you gave any trouble.'

The kitchen door is here, the stove is here, Aunty Doris is here and my grandmother is here. 'Ah, here, do you want some more? What don't you like about it? Too much salt, you always complain about my cooking. Aren't you having any, Mary? Manuel, here, you are too skinny. Paul, what don't you like about it?, is it eggs?, what's wrong with eggs, it's eggs. Just because of the way it looks, just eat it. These kids, fussy. He's fussy, they're fussy, everyone is fussy, I don't know why I bother. Mary, have some. Paul, eat it. Alright, I will make you something else. Next time if you don't like my cooking make it yourself. Here. Paul, help me with the plates, help me wash, come on.'

I would. But not my brother Manuel. We were here and here. Facing each other and trying not to look at each other. I was too scared to do anything with Grandfather at the table. It was rare that my brother and I fought. I had more trouble with my cousin, if she came. She'd go [*twitching nostrils*] and that would be the end of me, and my grandfather would go, 'Get out! Get out! Get out!'

'Can I have some more lemonade?'

'No, lemonade is no good for you, all that bloody sugar gives you asthma.'

'Who said that, Mary?'

'A friend of mine told me up the road.'

'Which friend?'

'He told me it gives him asthma.'

'Well, that's bloody ridiculous, never heard anything so stupid in my life.'

'I'll bring them, Nan, I'll bring the plates. I'll wash up.'

'See how he helps Nanna, why don't you help?'

'Because I don't fucking want to.'

'Don't swear.'

'Well, I don't want to.'

'Well, you should do something to help Mum around the bloody house. Alright, I'm going out.'

'You going to the club, Doris?'

'No, I don't like going to that bloody Maltese Club, frigging wogs.'

'Do you want anything else? I made some rice pudding. I just made it. Oh, come and have some rice pudding, I know he likes the rice pudding. Ah, there is plenty, I will go and get it for you. Here. Alright, I will sit down for a minute, but I have got to do the washing-up. You working tomorrow, Lonz?'

'Of course I am working. Isn't that what I normally do, work?' [*He slurps.*]

'Oh, yummy rice pudding yummy I love rice pudding it's my favourite. Yippee! Yippee!'

'I'll take some for Sam 'cause he likes it. Alright youse, I am going now. Manuel, better behave or I will smack you. And don't run around because you will get an asthma attack and don't talk to strangers out the front, there are men who'll show their penis. There are men waiting to show you their penis.'

'Which men Mummy, which men?'

'Just men, men, any man standing there, just don't go on your own.'

'Ej jien qatt ma nhallihom johorġu wahidhom.' ['Ay, I never let them go out on their own.'] 'I always watch them. After five minutes they have to come back.'

'Yes, well nothing better happen to my kids.'

'Well, if you don't bloody like it take them with you, why should my frigging mother and frigging father look after your bloody kids?'

'Mind your business bitch.'

'Hares, look, look. Stop. Shh. Shh. Oqghod.' ['Be quiet.']

'Ha. Get out. Get out! Get out!'

I am trying to remember if my mother smoked at the table. I think she did. My grandmother smoked, but never around us. I only found out when I went to clean the post office with her and she did it in front of me. That was a place she could finally find some peace.

LEARNING TO WORK/LEARNING TO SING

Angela was a worker. She really believed in work. The first thing she saw when she came to Australia was a woman in a fur coat sweeping her front step. She said, *'Issa din qatt ma tiġri f'Malta'.* 'Now that would never happen in Malta. A woman in a fur coat wouldn't sweep, she would have someone to sweep for her.' So it didn't take long until she got a job. There was a Hungarian Jew, Mr Vunha, around the corner who had a meat salad business. She worked for him for many years and got lots of Maltese women jobs too. They'd cut up the meat and mix mayonnaise into it. I used to have it on my sandwiches at school. She told me it was important for her to have her own money. My grandfather didn't like her working but she had a theory it was best to have money in case he left her. She said to him, *'Dawk l-flus tiegħi,'* ['That money is mine,'], 'you pay all the bills and the rent and this money will be for me and the kids'. She said to me it was because men being what they are he could take off. 'Even in Malta, in those days?' *'Iva,'* ['Oh yes,'], 'it is a big scandal, but it happens'. I think she just liked her independence.

When she was fourteen my mother started working in the factory where they made showbags. As kids we were obsessed with the Easter Show and those bags with lollies and toys in them. She would bring them home. They were fabulous. We would go, 'Oh!'; and then: nothing in them. And she would go, 'Yes, well, that's the bags'.

The last job Angela had was cleaning the Surry Hills post office. She used to go early in the morning and hose the front step and clean the windows and at night she would clear the rubbish, do the vacuuming and polish the lino. And I went with her because I needed to be everywhere she was. And I didn't like her being over there on her own at night. So I cleaned with her and that's when I started singing. I'd make these noises [*singing like a child*] and at first she would say, *'Madonna, inti tagħmilli uġiegħ ta' ras'* ['Oh my God, you are giving me a headache']; but later, 'You are getting better, you can sing'. I'd sing Judy Garland or Janis Joplin songs, and people would listen through the door. As people cleared their boxes, we would be on the other side. One day a man knocked at the window and said, 'Who's singing? Very nice voice.' And I went, 'Oh, it's my grandmother'.

NANNU

Paul holds a light switch.

My grandfather was a strong man. He was a big presence. He was an energy. He would get cranky. He was always exploding. If we pressed this switch more than once to turn off the lights it was, 'Hey!' And he had tattoos. He was a wharfie. I think he was jack of kids.

Maltese culture is very matriarchal but my grandfather took no nonsense. He and my grandmother fought, I remember them always arguing and fighting in Maltese. He didn't like her cooking. He used to cook for himself, he would be stirring the pot and he would pile on the chilli. He made his own chilli and pickled onions, and he used to eat this Maltese black meat sausage that revolted us. My grandfather was this big, scary thing but I could go up to him and say, 'Nannu, do you know where this place is, have you been there?' And he would say, 'Oh yes, I used to sell newspapers… Oh yes… Oh God, you know…' And that was my connection with him.

They never struck us, never hit any of the children. They didn't believe in hitting, so when Uncle Joe was hitting his sons, his mother-in-law told my grandmother. I was in the kitchen when she came over. And when Joe came in, my grandmother grabbed her own hair and pushed herself up against the wall and said, 'You mustn't hit them children'; and started banging her head against the wall, screaming, *'M'għandekx issawwat it-tfal, m'għandekx issawwat it-tfal tiegħek'.* ['Mustn't hit kids, mustn't hit your children'.] My grandmother had this habit, this thing she used to do and we would know it was absolutely the limit: she would bite her hand and leave an imprint; she would go [*making a sound*] and I did it too for a long time. If I got really beyond a point I would just [*repeating the sound*]. She would chase us around the table, *'Ejja hawn'.* ['Come here'.] My grandfather, he would just raise his voice. But he also made us laugh. 'Hey!'

My father had big problems coming to this country from Egypt. Greek-Egyptians had all these restrictions and coming to Australia in the 1950s, with girls in sexy clothes, he went berserk, just went off the rails to the horror of his parents, 'You're Greek and you have to marry a Greek'. And my father did absolutely the opposite. Impregnated my mother. HUGE SCANDAL. HUGE DISASTER. My father said me and my brother were both accidents. I was like, thanks, amazing I made it this far.

I always remember thinking as a child that I didn't belong anywhere. My grandparents were it. If it wasn't for them I don't know what would have happened to us.

Nannu got sugar diabetes. He was this big man and in a year he shrank to nothing. I will never forget it. He got an ear infection and had to have an operation. I saw him in the hospital. He just went down and down and then he was gone. At 69.

My grandmother went to see him one Saturday, like she did every day. When she arrived at the hospital, they said, 'Your husband passed away about an hour ago'. And the first thing my grandmother said was, *'X'ser ngħid lil uliedi?'* 'What am I going to tell my children?'

She wouldn't go to the funeral. I remember saying to Mum, 'Are you coming with us?'; and she said, 'No, no, I am staying with your grandmother'. And then Angela started screaming. Just as I was leaving. She was with all these Maltese women in her bedroom and she started screaming, *'Huwa kien raġel tajjeb'*. 'He was a good man'. She wore black for a long time. That was tradition.

NUTS ABOUT MALTA

Old-fashioned postcards from Malta are shown and passed around the audience.

When I was a kid, I couldn't meet a Maltese person without begging for a postcard like this. It was like getting gold. I can't tell you how much time I spent pouring over these things because I was fascinated by this place where my family came from. I tried to imagine: They are not from here, they are from somewhere else and this is what that somewhere else looks like. It was a magical place.

It was the buildings, combined with my grandmother's stories about how beautiful Malta was. She loved her home but would always say, 'We couldn't stay there, we were so poor and your grandfather got sick, after the War he got really ill'. She had to do all the work, she had five kids, and people were talking about this place called Australia.

A photograph is shown.

My grandfather's father died in the First World War. His submarine was damaged and they had to flood the bulkhead, and he drowned. I went to a kinesiologist once who said, 'Someone in your family, they're trapped, they're suffocating, I am getting that strongly'. This is a photo of him.

My grandfather's mother remarried. Her eldest son didn't get on with her new husband, so he moved to Australia. After the War, when my grandfather heard about Australia, he said, 'I have a brother there but I don't know how to contact him'. And they said, 'If he is in Sydney, all you have to do is send a letter to the Maltese Club. You just put his name, Maltese Club, Darlinghurst, Australia.' So he wrote, and his brother replied, 'Come out by yourself first because I don't know if you will like it. It's very different from Malta.' So that's what he did. And the letters to Angela kept arriving and they kept changing: 'Come and live here'; and then, 'No, I am coming back. I don't like it, you will hate it'; then, 'Sell everything'; and finally, 'This is it'.

A photograph is shown.

She got the first-ever assisted passage. This is a photograph of the ship. 1948. She came with five children. By herself. With one suitcase. Never even been on a ferry. Terrified of water.

A photograph is shown.

This is Angela's father, The Gardener. He was a very quiet man, hardly spoke. There are no photos of Angela's mother. There are no photos of Angela as a child, either.

A photograph is shown.

In fact this is the first photograph that was ever taken of her.

A photograph is shown.

Angela Bonnici, 1950s. Sydney, Australia.

Paul Capsis as Angela in the 2010 Griffin Theatre production in Sydney. (Photograph: Michael Corridore)

This one I like. My grandmother used to say, 'I lived here, see this street, just here; see that church, that's where your mother was christened, that's Gżira, and this is Sliema; here I used to walk every day to go shopping'. I used to imagine that boy was me and I was in Malta.

A photograph is shown.

This is the Mosta Church. It has the third biggest dome in the world. It was bombed in the Second World War. A bomb went through the roof but didn't explode. *'Miraklu.'* ['A miracle.'] The bomb is still there.

A photograph is shown.

This is the police station my grandmother reckons she took my uncle to warn him that he better not misbehave.

A photograph is shown.

This is the son of the cousin my grandmother went to live with when she was eight.

A photograph is shown.

This is the Orpheum.

A photograph is shown.

And that's the church my mother was christened in.

A photograph is shown.

That's my grandmother's brother and his wife. She was from the island of Gozo and she had a very funny way of speaking Maltese. They have an accent. They stretch their words, they elongate them like, 'How you going, mate?' She had a bit of a beard. Angela's brother was a religious fanatic. He had an altar in his home. He would have been a priest if he could, except he had to marry her.

A photograph is shown.

I love this picture. It is hand-tinted, as they did in those days. And there they are: the whole family. In Australia. My grandmother said it was hard getting my uncle to wear a suit. Charlie. The volatile one.

A photograph is shown.

The oldest man-made structure on the planet Earth is on the island of Gozo. It's called *Ġgantija*, meaning 'giants'. It was dedicated to the Goddess. They built the temple in the shape of the human body.

A photograph is shown.

There is a room in the head, one in the arm and another in the heart, and so on. You go to the different rooms to heal whatever it is that needs healing.

A photograph is shown.

That's Aunty Carmen's wedding, 1957, Angela's eldest daughter. At Sacred Heart Church in Darlinghurst. There is my mother, she was a bridesmaid. And my grandfather, that was his look, the way I remember him: solid. Carmen married the uncle of the singer Troy Cassar-Daley, who was half-Maltese, half-Indigenous.

A photograph is shown.

That's his grandmother, Mananni. She had 21 children. We called them *Il-Fniek*, The Rabbits. Maltese people give everyone nicknames. She was *Taċ-ċrieki*, The Ring Lady, and they were The Rabbits. Twenty-one children. Thirteen lived. She was a wonderful woman. And there's my darling Nanna in a dress she made herself.

I have a piece of that dress which I cut out when I was a child. From the hem where it couldn't be seen.

Paul shows a piece of the dress to the audience.

NANNU SHAVING

When he shaved, Nannu would have a round, old mirror he probably brought from Malta, a faded, rusty thing. And he would have his cup with an anchor in red, with the cake of soap in it to make the cream.

He demonstrates.

He would have his metal blade, he'd flick the top off, and he would sit with his old bristle brush. I was fascinated by this ritual. *'Mur barra biex tilgħab, mur barra!'* 'Go out and play, go outside!' Sometimes he wore shorts, and he would sit there in his shorts and his balls would fall out. He used to sit out the front of the house to watch people with his legs spread and his balls hanging out for all the world to see.

He demonstrates.

He was always working, always. You never saw him watch TV, relax, always working, fixing, painting, sanding, climbing ladders, fixing gutters, he never stopped. It was like there was never a completion, because if that room was finished then there was something else that needed doing.

Working, working. Once we went down to the wharves to see him. He wore grey overalls, and had a truck, a grey truck in that late-'50s style. I always wanted to get into that truck but I never did.

My grandparents didn't like buying things so I played with leaves in the yard when I was a kid. I was obsessed with my grandfather's lemon tree. From the kitchen he could see if I was going to touch the flowers. I'd pretend they were chickens, I'd be going to play with them and, 'Hey!' So I had to find a leaf on the ground to play with. The yard was never a yard, it was a world, it was cities and countries. The bit in the middle was Malta and the bit on the side was Greece 'cause Dad was from Greece and I remember getting the big bricks and pretending to bomb Greece. I would bomb ants. They were the people running for the shelter and I would kill them with the bombs from the Germans. The cement was the water and I would spend hours with a ship because, 'It's a long journey'. I never played with Manuel. Except when we went to our Greek grandmother's. I wasn't allowed to talk to myself at her place. She would see me out the back of the yard pretending I was in Greece or Egypt, and she would go [*clapping his hands*], 'Talk to your brother! Play together.' Nannu was just happy that I wasn't making any noise. Or touching his plants.

TRANSITION:

Għana, a type of Maltese folk song, plays: 'Iż-Żaqq'.

Paul sings.

> *Kull ma tara trid tixtrih*
> *Sabiex f 'żaqqek tmur tpoġġieh*
> *X'kastiġ għandek kemm hu kbir*
> *Pu għalik kemm int ħanżir.*

Spoken by Paul between verses:

Din hija kanzunetta
folkloristika Maltija
Dwar tiekol ħafna ikel.
Huwa sejjaħ 'Iż-Żaqq' – 'L-istonku'.

This is a Maltese folk song
about eating too much food.
It's called *'Iz Zug'*—'The Stomach'.

The song continues.

> *Karawett, ful, qastan, lewż*
> *Ġellewż, ċiċri anke ġewż*
> *Narak tiekol ta' kull ħin*
> *X'marda għandek x'waħda din.*

Spoken by Paul:

'Jiena sejjer, Jiena sejjer il-Bingo.
Ħares lejn dawk il-platti. Għadhom barra.
Ikolli nagħmel kollox jien hawnhekk.
Jiena għidt sejjer barra!'

'I'm going out. I'm going to Bingo.
Look at them plates!
They are still out.
I have to do everything around here by myself.
I said I'm going out!'

BINGO

I followed her everywhere. I used to go with her to Bingo at Air Force House in Foster Street. She would smoke and leave the cigarette in her mouth.

He demonstrates.

She had this thing my grandfather made for her, a solid piece of wood to lift the card up, so it was easy for her to mark.

He demonstrates.

People would go, *'Min fejn ġibtha dik?'* ['Where did you get that from?'] 'My husband made it for me.' She would have her crayon and a cigarette in her mouth and Clarrie would be calling, 'Legs 11, double 1, 5, 5 only, 66, clickety-click'. Clarrie the Bingo caller, '55, double 5, 1, 1 only'. I would sit on the table and the place was full of smoke but I didn't care as long as I was with my grandmother.

She won sometimes: 'Yeah!', and I'd jump up, because everything would be quiet when she was getting close. *'Ejja numru 16'* ['Come on number 16'], 'number 16, 16', and I would go, 'Oh my God', and I would get all excited, my heart would beat really fast. 'Yeah!' Twenty-five dollars was the most you could win. She loved it. Then she said, 'At your age, you should get a job like the other boys'. She taught me how to give change. She would go, 'If a card costs five cents and I give you 20 cents how much do you have to give me back?' And I would be like '… 15?' 'Yeah.' Well, it was all very well and good in the yard but come time to do the job I started to cry. My first day I only got to four people and the game was over. I cried and Clarrie went, 'Get that boy out of here, get that crying child out of here'. Anyway, eventually I got good and did it for years and they paid us two dollars per night. I started saving money and my grandmother would watch everything I brought into the house. If I brought in a magazine, *'X'ghandek hemmhekk'* ['What you got there'], 'what's that rubbish, waste of money, you look at it and then what, you throw it away'. That's how I was drilled daily.

I felt very lucky. I had this nightlife with my grandmother. Other kids were at home doing their homework or watching TV. And I was going off to Bingo. It finished at ten o'clock and we'd run to get the bus. I'd be scared that she might fall over because once she fell on her knees and I remember feeling the pain of her falling. Her Maltese friends would say to her, *'Inti għandek xortik tajba, inti għandek n-neputi tiegħek'* ['You are so lucky, you have got your grandson'], 'he goes everywhere with you, I wish my grandson would do that', and she would say to them, 'Don't give me bad luck, say praise be to God when you say that because I don't want anything to happen'.

MANUEL

Paul stands by cupboard. A photograph of Lonz is shown.

My brother used to get asthma really badly and have to go to St Vincent's Hospital. So there was a time when I was six or seven, and there was just me and my grandfather at home. I was watching television. My grandfather came in and said, 'It's too late now to watch TV, turn it off'. I was in the room alone, in pitch black darkness, absolutely petrified. I went into the hall and lay down on the floor outside his bedroom and just knowing he was there, I felt safe. He must have heard me because he opened the door and said, *'Isa, isa, idħol fis-sodda'* ['Come on, come on, back to bed'], and I went to bed and he turned on the TV and lay next to me.

POSTCARD FROM MALTA II

Paul lights candles. An audio-visual of Malta being bombed is projected onto the cupboard.

Six thousand seven hundred tons of bombs fell on Malta just in April of 1942. Supply ships were attacked, people began to starve. The daily ration was three boiled sweets, half a sardine and a spoonful of jam.

When I think of Malta I think of the buildings, the houses, the balconies, the flat roofs, the sandstone itself. But primarily I think of the churches. I think of the big Mosta Church.

It's huge. If you are standing across the road from it, it is actually difficult to take in. To photograph it I have to take two pictures. It has a huge circular dome made of limestone. There are columns at the front, in the classical style. Inside it's very simple. Because of the dome, there's intense light. I feel an overwhelming awe. The size of the church is extraordinary. Lots of light and air, caught. There is a mosaic of Jesus going to the heavens, and an opening at the very top which allows the light to spill through. Throughout the church there are long brass candle-holders, and red velvet hangings. And there is a little shop that sells postcards, crosses and beads.

Outside it is dry and hot, but in a pleasant way. There is a little pizza shop. There are tables and chairs and a counter with people waiting. They are all very similar, the men in particular. They have got dark skin and look at me as if I am one of them. They are dressed in board shorts and sunglasses and gold crosses. They seem sure of themselves and slightly aggressive, good-looking. They are talking loudly and joking. There is a girl who could be a sister or a wife sitting in the back quietly.

I am really happy to be here. I feel the connection to my history, my ancestors, my family. Like I am home. A place I know.

Now I am in the Upper Baraco Gardens in Valetta, overlooking the Grand Harbour, and you can see the old fortress across the water. The Grand Harbour is breathtaking. The gardens are beautiful, simple and very old. There are ships docking and you can just see to the other side. The water is blue, blue, blue, clear water, and there is the green of the gardens. The colours are amazing. It could be any time, it could be 1943, it could be 1843. Everything is as it's always been.

There are lots of stairs and I climb down to the bottom to where the boats dock. I look to my right and see a tiny door and it's open. I go inside and it's like a cave, with candles burning. It's a room where people sheltered in the War because it was so deep under the city. It is perfectly preserved and just lit with candles.

When the bombings started people found refuge wherever they could. They dug into the sandstone. Into the bedrock of Malta was cut a warren of honeycombed rooms—offices, dormitories, even one for giving birth.

I sense all the people in there praying, praying, *'Marija għinni, Ġesù għinni. Mulej għinni—inħalli f'idejk.'* ['Help me Mary, help me Jesus. If it pleases you—help me, God.'] 'Please help, please don't let the bombs drop here.' It is very small, but there is a spirit here. This is a place of safety, it's safe.

PAUL, NOW

When things are at their worst people say, 'How are you going?' And I say, 'I am experiencing life, I am experiencing life fully'. Death, betrayal, people disappearing, friendships fading. I'm like, 'Wow, this is how it is'. And it just keeps going like this.

Death can't be helped. That's how it is. The important thing for me was my grandmother, the most important thing of all. I knew it would be from the very first time my uncle Gary, the Aussie footballer, the philosopher, told me about it. As a five-year-old I didn't know death existed. I said, 'What does that mean, "die", what is "die"?' He said, 'Well, one day we stop breathing and they put us in the ground'. And I looked at him and he went, 'You know, like one day Nanna will die'. He picked her as the example. And my life was never the same. I remember praying to God, 'Please let me die first. Let me die before her'; and I never forgot that prayer.

I used to play with little plastic animals in the garden. My cousins would go on about it. They'd go, 'Oh, I remember you and them animals; you'd bury them; God, you're weird'. Until then, the animals were getting married and having babies. Now they were dying too.

THE MYTHICAL FAMILY

Paul holds a family album from which he reads.

Angela's family numbers sixty-four people.
I call them my Mythical Family.

Angela's mother Rosie was married to a Maltese whose name was Tony. He was a gardener, so I call him The Gardener.

They had six children, three of whom survived: Tony, Petrina and Angela herself. One sister died from eating limestone from the church walls.

Angela married Annunciato, who was called Lonz. To me they are Nanna and Nannu. They had seven children: Charlie, Carmen, Tonina, Teresa, Mary, my mother, Joe and Doris, the youngest.

Charlie married Maree, an Irish Australian, and they had five children: Wendy, Louise, Katarina, Dean and Sally. Wendy had four sons: Nigel, George, Anthony and Glen. Louise had one son, David, Katarina one son, Micky, Dean one son, Stuart, and Sally one son, Matthew.

Carmen married Johnny, and they had four daughters: Jan, Linda, Cathy and Lisa. Jan married a half-Aboriginal man and had two sons. Linda had three daughters, one son, and five grandchildren. Cathy had three daughters. She has a granddaughter, half-Maori. Lisa had two daughters and one son.

Tonina died when she was two-and-a-half.

Teresa married Sal and they had two children: Abigail and Steve. Abigail had two sons: Tommy and Nigel. Steve had a daughter: Bec.

Joe married a Greek Cypriot, Dora, and they had two sons: Brett and Darren. Brett had two daughters: Jill and Nicola. Darren had one son: Dean.

Doris married an Australian, Gary, who I call The Blonde God, and had three children: Alan, Kevin and Tracey, who had, respectively, one daughter, two sons, and one son.

Mary, my mother, married my father Chris, a Greek Egyptian. They were married for less than two years and had two sons: Manuel and me, Paul.

Seven children. Eighteen grandchildren. Thirty-three great-grandchildren. Seven great-great-grandchildren.

Voice: Kemm mietu mill-familja? [How many of the family died?]

Eight.

Voice: Kemm hemm dawk li huma fuq d-droga? [How many became drug addicts?]

Three.

Voice: Kemm huma dawk li marru joqogħdu fil-Punent? [How many moved out West?]

Eleven.

Voice: Kemm huma dawk li marru lura biex iżuru Malta? [How many went back to visit Malta?]

Three, me being the first.

Voice: Kemm huma dawk li huma omosesswali? [How many are gay?]

Two.

Voice: Kemm huma dawk li huma reliġjużi? [How many are religious?]

One.

Voice: Kemm huma dawk li huma sinjuri? [How many are rich?]

Three.

Voice: Kemm huma dawk li huma kuntenti? [How many are happy?]

Three.

Voice: Kemm huma dawk li żaru lil Angela fil-ġimgħat qabel ma mietet? [How many visited Angela in the weeks before she died?]

Twenty-six.

Voice: Minn kemm-il pajjiż huma ġejjin dawn? [How many countries do they come from?]

Ten.

Teresa's son, Steve, died as a result of heroin, when he was 32 years old. I look like him. Of all my cousins, he and I looked the most similar.

We heard he got married, but none of us were invited to the wedding. He was covered in tattoos, completely, his whole arm like a sleeve. He was skinny. Long hair, a very quiet person.

He rode into a cement pole on a pushbike and snapped his spine. I went to see him laid out in the hospital, tattoos, in a coma. The funeral was one of the worst funerals I have ever been to. They played Death Metal. Steve's wife was an addict too. A year later they found her overdosed in a public lavatory. She was buried with him.

Recently I bought some paints and canvases and as part of my healing I did these dot paintings. A dot represents a spirit, a person. The dots are slightly different for those who have passed on and those who are present, and still part of this mythical family.

Postcards of Malta are shown.

Paul sings a Maltese lullaby, a capella.

ANGELA IN AUSTRALIA

Paul begins clearing the stage.

Angela cried every day for the first two years after she came to Australia. Because of the language, the culture, the way people were. Maltese are very social. She said, 'Here everyone is in their little houses'. Her neighbour in Riley Street would say, 'Bloody dagoes, speak English'.

Angela said if you could physically do five jobs you could get five jobs in Australia. I'd say, 'But, Nan, you had all them kids'. The fear of poverty never left her. I would say, 'We are not in Malta now, the War's over'. And she'd go, 'Ohhh, but you never forget. When there nothing to eat, you have nothing to eat.'

Once I went over to visit her and I said, 'This house is freezing, Nan, what's with this no heater stuff? I can't even take off my coat. This is not good for you.' And she would go to me, 'You waste, you love wasting electricity. Look, I put three jumpers on and five scarves, I have got my warm slippers and I am going to go to bed. I am not cold.'

With Angela, it was that thing of do without, do without, do without. We bought her a new TV. She punched the cupboard, she was so upset. She shouted at me, 'I told you, I told you I didn't want it, but nobody listens to me'. Anyway, eventually she learnt to use the remote, but it was difficult. She said, 'Easy for you, you have education, I never had education, you say press the button, I don't know what it means "the button", I don't understand "the button"'.

She was an absolutely devout Catholic. At church every Sunday. The whole family went, except my grandfather. When I was in my teens, and in a rebellious stage, I would say, 'But, Nan, Grandpa doesn't go'. 'He's a man,' she would say, 'he'll have to face God later'.

GOING BACK TO MALTA

I wonder about Angela going back to Malta. Whether it would have broken her heart. Because absolutely everything has changed.

There were lots of Maltese who had gone back, and they would say, 'Oh, Malta, it's expensive'; or 'It's crowded'. She'd argue with them, 'Oh no, Malta is not like that, no they don't do that in Malta'. And someone who had just got back would say, 'But I am telling you, I was just there'. She would say, 'Did you see the bakery? Opposite the house.' 'I don't remember a bakery, I saw an alley with a little door.' 'Yes, that's the bakery, that's where you go in.' Nineteen forty-eight was the last time she was there.

WHEN IT COMES TO MONEY, EVERYTHING CHANGES

My grandmother and I had this big fantasy about the family. She loved that I got on with everybody, but in truth there were a lot of problems. Some of them didn't speak to each other. They never gathered, never celebrated her birthday. A lot of them saw her only once a year. They weren't really close, if I'm honest. When she was in the hospice and I was around them, I felt very alone.

Angela was happy to see her kids get on and marry and buy homes, but the thing was, most of them went to live far, far away from her. This isn't normal in Maltese culture. They moved away so she didn't see her grandchildren.

Paul goes behind the cupboard to change.

As he speaks, Angela's photograph is shown.

The day after my grandmother died, I went over to Aunty Carmen's for lunch. I walked into the house and out to the yard. And my uncles, at the top of their voices, were talking about contesting the Will. I froze. One uncle was saying, 'You can't contest what Mum wants'. 'Yes you can, you can bloody contest it, of course you can. You fucking better.' And I thought, "My grandmother died yesterday, she's frozen in ice, and they are talking about the Will", and I wanted to pick up the table with the food and throw it and smash everything in the house and leave.

Paul reappears as Angela.

Isn't it funny? They all united. I said to Mum, 'If only they had put that energy into celebrating her life, just once'. My grandmother used to worry about them getting together. She would say, *'U le, iz-zijiet tiegħek jistgħu jibdew għlieda.'* 'Oh no, your uncles might start a fight.' But when it came to her money, they bonded.

LAST THINGS

One of the last times I took my grandmother out she went to see a Maltese friend who had become housebound like her. She said, *'Ħares lejna, ħares lejn din il-ħajja fl-Awstralja eh, dejjem ġewwa bħall-klieb'.* ['Look at us, look at this life in Australia, eh, always inside like dogs.'] 'Maltese our age, they could walk around the street, you could just walk out your front door and see someone and have a chat. Here the people stay in their houses like dogs.' They were talking in Maltese. They were both going, 'Isn't this a strange country?' After spending most of their lives here.

My mother didn't go to Angela's funeral. She fed my grandmother in the hospital. When the doctors called us in to say Angela was shutting down my mother didn't want to know. I said, 'Mum, you cannot feed Nanna anymore, she can't swallow'. Mum didn't say goodbye. She left the hospital and never went back. I said to her, 'You have to go to the funeral because it is going to help you grieve'. She said, 'No, no, no, no'.

WHEN ANGELA GOT SICK

Had I known what was going on with Angela, had the diagnosis been made before I left for New York that she had stage four lung cancer, I couldn't have gone. There is no way in the world.

Pause.

I was working there when my cousin rang to say Nanna was dying. Because Mum wasn't telling me, no-one was telling me.

Pause.

They said, 'We will only give you this amount of time to go'. I called my manager. She said, 'You have to make a decision, do you see her alive or do you go to her funeral?' When I rang Angela from New York to say I was coming home, she said, 'Don't you dare, you have a job to do', and when I arrived she was cross. The first thing she said was, *'Inti ma smajtx minni'.* ['You didn't listen to me'.] 'I told you not to come back, but you didn't listen'.

I was with her when she passed away. I was next to her holding her right arm. I was the first to notice her breathing had changed.

Pause.

After I got back from New York I went alone to the grave, and it was very difficult. I just couldn't fathom she was in there, I just couldn't believe it. I feel her so strongly, I see her, I hear her, her voice. I think about her a lot because for me she was the centre, the rock. No matter what was going on in my life, if I just stood with my grandmother, just stood next to her, I felt instant safety.

SOME OLD, WRECKED, PRECIOUS THINGS

Paul folds the table into a suitcase. He holds up one object after another, putting them away.

This is the blanket she held over her knees when she watched television. The light switch. The thing she used to rest her hand on at Bingo. The jumper she knitted for me. Her shoes, the last pair she wore. The remote control for her TV.

Paul holds up a book.

This book is my connection to Malta. It's an old library book and I stole it.

The book's name is *Paul Is A Maltese Boy*. It used to have a smell about it. It still does, sort of.

My grandmother could relate to every picture. 'Now this is Valetta and that's the old Opera House here. Your grandfather used to sell newspapers on the steps when he was about nine.' This all got bombed, all of it. Now there's nothing. I have looked.

Look at it.

Paul holds up the book.

This little, old, wrecked, precious thing.

The suitcase is closed, and the handle added. Paul places it centre stage and sits on the edge of it.

POSTCARD FROM MALTA III

A panorama of Malta's Grand Harbour is shown.

Now I am in Sliema. The sun is going down and I can see the water changing colour. The sky is golden and all the buildings are shimmering. There are people promenading and it's very slowly getting darker and the lights start flickering on. There is just beautiful, bouncing light off the water, the golden sun and people.

There are people with babies in prams. There are lots of couples. There are older people with their children. There is noise from cars, beeping and shouting, but it doesn't seem to affect the walkers, they just keep walking slowly. There are young men shouting at each other out of their car windows. I can hear young kids screaming and laughing. It's a whole other world.

Kif npoġġi fuq il-ajruplan u nhares mit-tieqa nipprova nilmaħ liċċkejkna Malta u nipprova ma nħallihiex għaddejja. As I board I try to get a glimpse of the island, not wanting to let it go. I sit there listening to people, trying to catch a Maltese accent or someone speaking in Maltese. Then we pull away and I look, desperate for a last sight of an island, a tiny island, a sandstone island and think, "That can't be Malta because it's too small." *"Din ma tistax tkun Malta għaliex hija żgħira wisq."* And I just catch the top and some of the coast *u nipprova żżommha sakemm ikun possibbli. Sakemm ikun possibbli.* And I try and hold onto it as long as possible.

Pause.

As long as possible.

THE END

www.ingramcontent.com/pod-product-compliance
Lightning Source LLC
Chambersburg PA
CBHW041935090426
42744CB00017B/2070